FERN HOLLOW

Richard Blevins

*Alfred Jarry once wrote that in order to dwell
in eternity, one has only to experience two separate
moments at the same moment.*
—Gerald Murnane, "First Love"

SPUYTEN DUYVIL

New York

Library of Congress Cataloging-in-Publication Data

Names: Blevins, Richard, author.
Title: Fern hollow / Richard Blevins.
Description: New York : Spuyten Duyvil, [2023]
Identifiers: LCCN 2023012938 | ISBN 9781959556213 (paperback)
Subjects: LCGFT: Poetry.
Classification: LCC PS3503.L635 F47 2023 | DDC 813/.54--dc23/eng/20230324
LC record available at https://lccn.loc.gov/2023012938

to Dodo Marmarosa

OLIVIER MESSIAN

JOHN JAMES AUDUBON

FLANNERY O'CONNOR

HUEY LONG

LORINE NIEDECKER

FERN HOLLOW

To Leon Cadore

It is in a spirit of no confidence in myself,
or I mean in the human race,
that I have taken bird-songs as model.
—Olivier Messiaen to Antoine Goléa

I can remember for a long time

　　　　　　　vaguely thinking I was missing out

on a big part of my life because I couldn't remember actually watching

a sunrise happen

　　　　and there are only so many.

　It dawned on my melatonin'd mind that I needed to

　　　　　　　prioritize.

That was before sciatica

had me up walking the floor every morning, already rewriting "Hyperion"

　　　　　just out of bed. Too early in the day to desire an art so perfect

　　　　　as Keats' enfolding poems in letters to America

along with a theory of poetry

that reads like a letter home

with great poems occurring like transcribed birdsongs,

　　　　　　　not so much true to life as they are life,

inside Messiaen's

articulations.

As Norman Demuth observed: Even birds have to take a breath!

The same bird at different times of day.

His form is episodic, not the symbolic song of the nightingale of Jannequin, Couperin, Beethoven,
Stravinsky.

Messiaen's seven-volume *Traité de Rythme, de Couleur et d'Ornithologie*, compiled 1949 to d., most resembles Audubon's *The Birds of America*. There he portrays the nightingale's song as "repeated low pitches each preceded by a grace note, and then concluding with a flourish," onomatic "tio, tio, tio, tiotiolaborix" (Kraft). Like Keats, Messiaen often wrote birdsong rhythm in iambic feet.

      Also silences like dark bushes entangling sleeping birds

if you've ever held a bird in your hands, the throb of a faster life entrusted, and felt like Keats procrastinating. Reading has invented the songbirds Keats knew: the singing bird creates nothing new, the bird remains

          true to bird language filling his tiny body

          with the new sun, tho the singer's bones, meant for flight,

are hollow
prisoners' bones.

Grace notes are feathers.

Allen Shawn writing music from Bennington, wrens on a bench, knowing that The End of the World is not the end of the world but the vista of graduation into the world the banal can't kill. And that is all ye need to know. (It will embarrass him to read this but) his work has given me this poem: no flight of fancy but the long haul to Vermont, and arrival.

I cannot stand to listen
the prisoners of meter reciting
their beloved Audubon, his
"shot a bird,
wired it up,
and drew" verses make me claustrophobic.
Our turn to stand in the field near Nancy,
Americans, wooden shoes
keep our
feet warm—
Quartet for the End of Dance is about to premier

"But what truly pushes [*Pierrot Lunaire*] over the edge into the world of the sublimely bizarre is how that music combines with the singer who isn't quite singing." (Shawn)

"...there is no realism possible in music (discounting the actual

A sod counting ghost notes,

I stand with Le Boulaire, the atheist violin, who was the last to leave the stalag, who gave up the
violin for an acting career under the name Lanier, who starred as Cocteau's Oreste.
We are prisoners, but the field is open—"amid all the severity, suddenly, a song would arise," Le B
remembered, the one in the quartet unclouded by religion.
This is not realism but actual flight.

<blockquote>"bird calls in Messiaen's music or
the use of sounds from daily life…"</blockquote>

for spring, the types of sonnets became odes, tiny blue and brown eggs in a kerchief; by fall, the
unrimed sonnet is yet a sonnet declaring it open season 125 years before the Kingfisher poem.
for the Nightingale's eighth stanza, Keats' breaks the iambic jam and the unrimed sonnet remains
a sonnet Spring is a harvest time. it is open season. Jesus, Olson's kingfisher is older than me.
Meanwhile. Underwater, the Poseidon sea

In Bennington, I always took a motel
three blocks from the care home
where Carl Ruggles died of old age,
the first years without knowing;
after that I visited Crescent only
the one time.

grass meadow has been growing! Its birds are fish.
All the many rules about poesy only apply to poems
that copy forms. The two sonnet types fold into the ode
he is mixing. By 1959, Messiaen birdsongs transcend
all musical tradition. No harps in all of his oeuvre.
Birds are the voices of God.
This world is a tall tree of birds getting started
before the sun calls ("getting up with the birds,"
Mom called it), or going to bed ("with the chickens").
Loaded up on harmolodics at breakfast today.

How many Robert Frost houses
are there north of Boston?
I found Carl Ruggles'
first try.

Gary Giddens' elements of harmolodics: OC's "privileged ear resisted the laws of harmony, melody, rhythm, and pitch…Melody: What will it sound like if it follows its own course, free of harmonic premises? Rhythm: What is four/four but an artificial subset of one/one, and who says we have to submit to it? Pitch: Screw the tempered scale and the lute it rode in on."
[OM in 1958: "Suppose that there were a single beat in all the universe. One beat; with eternity before it and eternity after it. A before and an after. Imagine then…a second beat. Since any beat is prolonged by the silence which follows it, the second beat will be longer than the first. Another number, another duration. That is the birth of Rhythm."] (R.S. Johnson)

Ornette's "Skies of America" (1972/2022)

This is on my mind. To stop even. Just as the rhythm. Just.
—Robert Duncan, "A Book of Resemblances"

OM described himself to Claude Samuel as "an ornithologist and a rhythmician." In OM's opera, scene 6, Saint Francis understands the language of bird and speaks his song to them. The composer made the trip to New Caledonia to hear for himself the song of the Philemon (Friarbird).

Early on, in *Poèmes pour Mi*, "many birds are represented with contrasting rhythmic patterns to the other birds that surround them."
OM hunted birds' "natural rhythmic complexity. Birds never sing as part of an ensemble: the dawn chorus is not heard as a homogenous ensemble, but as a continuous cacophony of individual songsters." (Kraft)

Most resembles *Skies of America* when the conductor signals hors tempo and the birdsong players play their own time independent from the orchestra.

Resemble Assembly

A constantly moving.—Robert Duncan, "A Book of Resemblances"

The plash of rain this
morning. The birds
inside me nesting.

I am Jean Lanier.
In no way do I
resemble

Jean Lanier
when I am not
writing.

He was tall; big French
voice. Most importantly,
he is out of time.

Resemblance is frequently misleading.
Whatever was Dorthe Nors doing
here in my Laundromat

and not back in Jutland
keeping dry in her room?
If the woman resembling

Dorthe Nors inch-square
author's photograph
on the paperback

A Line in the World
really is unaware of the
resemblance

then why does she only
pretend to be reading at the
laundromat? She should go

to the café
or bookstore
to read like me.

I will call her Dorthe,
holds it up to hide her face
so I don't get a good look

Please, may I
take our
photograph?

How long ago the kids made faces.
Made fun of my big wazoo,
Blevin the Baptist Jew,

rimes with
"style oiseau,"
you hick shits!

shame pain
can still sting. After 70,
I no longer much

resemble
myself. I am no longer
a popular classroom teacher.

Twice divorced, I live alone.
What's the percentage
for a bat in Tod's house in Maine

and a bat in Mathilda's room in Pennsylvania
on the same day:
his attic, her basement?

A bat is not a bird but
bird-like as in
an interrupting nightmare.

It's hard to sleep with a bat
when it isn't flying. There
is no living with it, finally.

It is not like living among wild
birds. It only resembles a bird.

Messiaen couldn't use gramophone
records for his birdsong transcriptions
since, like a snapshot of a person,
they convey only part of a song.

Audubon once had a dead child
disinterred so he might give the parents
a likeness "as if still alive,"

a resemblance. Maybe it put him to sleep
                eventually to imagine
being zipped tight
                                inside the foliage of a tree asleep on his feet
    on a branch.
The leaves contracting and expanding

a bower slowly breathing, the

          other birds around him silent

counting out

ghost notes.

[II]

Never saw so many sunrises! And no two alike.

Never took in so many dawn choruses!

When I crack open the window, the birds come in.

I mean, the sounds

of birds.

Before long, I must shut up

the house against the day's heat. The

choir has knocked off for the time

being anyway.

If you read Keats long enuf, the sun comes up again

the progress of the wall I write against is interrupted

by an open window, and encouraged by a framed picture

the book left open on my table makes puns

until I bother to shut the window and

its leaves cease blowing.

I do not need to read the underlined passages in the book that describe

the picture since I have done the hard work of memorizing them.

The frame dissolves for a time during work.

Without looking up from my work I know the landscape below the

window is alive again with birds more than happy to wear surgical masks

First the Mourning Dove

it was her cry that brot Spring

so she is never tired

of taking credit

a fine mist unscrolls

revealing figures in conversation

eating their own words

too bad there can be no freedom from this hunger

Food!

     Food!

          Food!

their song blows back at them, my hand is in the process of morphing into a gnarl of wood, a Woodpecker makes my hollow head its nest, peers out thru my eye sockets—

"…and I put it into a wooden cage, every part of which it examined, until finding a spot by which it thought it might escape; it began to work there, and soon made the chips fly off. In a few minutes, it made its way out, and leaped upon the floor, uttering its common *cluck*, hopped to the wall, and ascended as if it had been on the bark of one of his favorite trees. The room being unfinished, the bricks were bare, and as it passed along, it peeped into the interstices, and seized the spiders and other insects which it found lurking there. Remarking often his looking under the cracks and the little shelves in the rough wall, I drew him in that position."

The caged bird is a point of unity in Melville's film, along with the assassin's creased hat.
Mocking American killers.

"A couple of times on the tape, there is a terrible SLAM. De Kooning explains the noise:
birds have been flying into the clear windows of his studio." (Ada Calhoun)

First time in my life, I can write in the early morning I am up
various times thru the night to pee and jot down lines for the poem (in the first movement of
Quartet for the End of Time, the clarinet-blackbird and the violin-nightingale awaken between 3-4
a.m.) then wake up for good about 5:00, ready to go like a kid out of school for the summer.
The birds of the dawn chorus are the only clock.

"Funny that you should ask about the birdscape
of Kent," Dean Keller writes from Ohio. "This year,
we made a list of what we saw:

Cardinal; Blue Jay; Chickadee;
Cedar Wax Wing; Nuthatch; Wren;
Cat Bird; Oriole; Woodpecker
(Downy, Hairy, Pileated, Red-
Bellied, Red-headed, Flicker);
Finch (a variety); Titmouse;
Junko; Sparrows (a variety);
Black Birds (a variety, including
Crow and Red Wing); and these
on the ground under the feeders—
Mourning Dove; Geese; Turkey;
Robin.

"Sort of reads like a poem!"

The one Messiaen piece containing only birdsong is *Oiseaux Exotiques*, commissioned by Boulez.
48 birdsongs, mostly from North America, also from South America, India, Malaysia, China,
and the Canary Islands. Hindu and Greek rhythms. The Magpie's "machine gun" effect and the
Catbird's "miaow."

Read Keats long enuf, and the sun sinks again.
Ohio more and more resembles Silesia.

[III]

Yesterday and / bird are gone—A.R. Ammons, "Tape for the Turn of the Year"

For one whole year the birdsongs are drowned
out by mean construction on the fallen bridge.
Fern Hollow makes the national news: the crane
operator swung the city bus to safety as everyone
held their breath. Then it dropped out of the cycle
and became a permanent detour. I drew the drapes
and shut my window. Things had changed next time
I opened it. Trees that could only be designed by
Mondrian and found in the old Carnegie. It is strictly
forbidden for children to climb trees; swing requires
annotation. Do not walk on the grass. Do not feed
the birds. Whole trees full of birds are wired for
Spring like Christmas trees. Some families go all out—
I like the guy who leaves his birds up all year long so
he never has to take them down. Now that it's May,
they turn on the sun satellite one hour earlier every day
and start up the birdsong choir one hour before that.
Plenty of official nature nostalgia on my devices but
face prison if I'm caught with my copy of *The Birds of
America:* the book hides like a bat in the daylit house.
Recharged, I plug in my day. I applaud the improvements
they've made in the Avisbots, engineering greater variety
in birdsongs, but it's just not the same to wake up to pop
songs from Robert-Houdini's bird. I have to play my illicit
Messiaen over secret headphones lest neighbors turn me in.
I was out walking with my friend Mason in the barrens beyond
the surveillance cameras, when, without prelude, he deftly
shot one. I hadn't even know he was carrying. He is my
friend so we will stick to one story. It must have been a
difficult shot, surprising even himself. The Avisbot short
circuited in an electric flash and plunged sparks into weeds.

For the opera
Stravinsky's
mechanical
nightingale
doubles:
the dancers
mime
the hidden
singers.

I don't know the difference between species so Mason pointed
out how to distinguish a Chinese CL-901 from the Switchblade
he bagged. Shooting an Avis is very dangerous, just *having* one
is a punishable offense, but Mason being a painter took it home
no matter. Around here, poachers simply disappear. In their time,
the birds had never practiced, they had written no new music (or
what humans can hear as music: birds sing at a high pitch, up to
17,000 Hz; the highest note on OM"s piano was 4,000), those birds
never just felt like not singing today. They remained till their last
day unaware of how many of them had died, within the last decade,
when immigrating birds slammed into skyscrapers. They hadn't
bothered to notice how insect populations are dwindling. The bird
parliament had no answers to Covid or Pokrasa or inflation or the rash of mass
shootings across America, dumb as Florence's mechanical dove Columbina
whose fireworks started Easters. Until 1999, when two children in
Hong Kong became infected with H9N2, a new strain of the virus,
avian flu was believed to spread from bird to bird only. Five years
later, the NIAID tasked Chiron Corporation to produce a vaccine.
The resulting vaccine was tested at Baylor, and results published
online in September 2006. The MF59 vaccine is licensed in Europe
but not in the US. Global Protection's Avian Flu Kit (consisting of
gloves, mask, coveralls, and 1 sanitizing wipe) is available for purchase
on eBay.

Within the plague
doctor's leather
beak, theriac is
burning, he inhales
the protective vape.

"I chose the birds—others, the synthesizer."—Messiaen

(Every bird

its own mode.)

No birds in

the air. I

don't dare

breathe. Drone

flocks.

(Messiaen felt the Willow Warbler's voice to be impossible to describe.)

One idea for

what's next

is move thru

the garden

statue-to-flowers,

grow increasingly

in love (a bird's

rapid heartbeat)

with creation.

(One track on *Skies of America* is called "Sounds of Sculpture.")

.

He could not have known the white statue-

bird of the stars

lets no one pass.

No one.

Correction for "I chose the birds…"
[At the last, the old composer
used Ondes Martenot.]

Migraine
Darkling I listen.

The sun bounces
                  off white paper and into my eyes, so
the birdsong will continue within
bedroom's pitch dark
                  illuminated
     by two migraine suns inside my head
when I close my eyes. Within a week,
I spied Audubon's
Bird of Washington and a Cuvier's
     Kinglet, without leaving home.

Eyes and Ears Specialist
Because I felt more comfortable at the start of *Schoenberg's Journey* where Shawn discusses the composer's paintings, I put on a CD and read the hard parts. "It should have *sung*, this 'new soul'—and not spoken!" (Nietzsche's Preface to *The Birth of Tragedy*, second edition) You read the language of flowers; hear the language of birds.

Milk and Dry Bread
"Everything speaks to me!   In faith
my sight is sound."—Duncan, Dante Etudes

The old man couldn't walk
                  without his notebook open.
He kept a bird

beneath his beret,

        birds walking

        awkwardly

  to stay

  among people,

  when flying

    comes easy.

Wrapped in the cloak of his disciplined faith, he enters

the woods without

missing a note

of birdsong, without knowing IF

that day's notation, or the matter of the week's notebooks,

might fit the new poem or how.

      Here and there

       to here and now.

A record of sounds he might have heard in the womb.

The sounds of words like the onoma of *tweet*.

He could always read his own handwriting, take

a Woodpecker home / under his cap. He held the bird

to his heart, something dying much faster than him.

And then

he got old, eyes and handwriting

gone to pot.

And now

he sees everything best

thru his ears.

The piano response, however nimble,

Cannot keep up

with the wren-flute

in the new Cadenza.

Songs keep just ahead of him, hop,

like a handful of breadcrumbs.

For M.C.B., her graduation day, May 28, 2022

PLENTY

But hopes are shy Birds flying at a great distance
seldom reached by the best of Guns.
—John James Audubon's Journal

Messiaen most closely resembles Audubon in the harmonies of his birdsongs.

Paul Griffiths observes that "Messiaen translates colours into harmonies, for those who have ears to see." (Kraft, p. 39)

It was my good fortune that the University of Pittsburgh owns one of the few complete copies of *The Birds of America*. Also by happenstance, Audubon came to draw the birds of western Pennsylvania. In 1824, Audubon was stranded for a time in Pittsburgh. Having walked the 90 miles down from Meadville, he found the Ohio River too low for his planned trip to Bayou Sarah. In Pittsburgh, he met the landscape artist George Lehman, of Lancaster, Pennsylvania, later hired to paint in perches and background habitats for *The Birds of America*.

Audubon's 435 paintings are mostly watercolors, with pastels, egg whites and pencil. (Note: the term "painting" is interchangeable with "drawing" for Audubon.) All drawings were done on Whatman paper.

Anybody else see
John Koehler's face
in John Syme's
portrait of Audubon?

The painter is
painted cradling his
rifle—of course,
John Francis Koehler

could never kill.
He might have
talked to backyard
rabbits toads snakes.

I see opera
belongs in the
Messiaen poem.
Resemblances can be

tricky, and nature's
plentitude is both
the prose poems of
A Book of
Resemblances
and Saint Francis'
Canticle of
Brother
Sun.

Duncan's sideburn'd visage
resembled a falcon's
when I knew
him. Even tho

by that time,
he disliked requests
to read again
the falcon poem.
(Did Poe bemoan his raven?)

And the Falcon
does not resemble
a songbird.
He wrote in

admiration of
Stravinsky
for the art
of not singing
like a bird.

His last year,
I saw him
read in Baltimore.
Suddenly, he was
an old man.

Once he got
to the podium,
birdcall never

wavered   (I never see
                                          the birds eat
                                          grass seed
for a minute.   from the old
                                          cat's grave.)
(It wounded him

when they called

him off after

two hours.)

It wounded Hart when Gatekeeper Crowe turned his back on him (in one fell swoop disavowing his own early best poems), stooping to be placed in high places, directing from the Kenyon lookout Duncan's Elegy to be stomped out before it started.

Crowe Ransom

had it all set up, perfectly, to his advantage—tuition for teaching his formal limitations— assisted by the author of *All the Kings Men* and fellow right-wing Fugitives.

Elected

Jones Very as our greatest poet.

[II]

The art registers   the kick of the gun.

"Nature," Emerson writes in "The Sovereignty of Ethics" essay, "is a tropical swamp in sunshine, on whose purlieus we hear the song of summer birds and see prismatic dew drops— but her interiors are terrific, full of hydras *and crocodiles*."

Florida Keys, 1832
Killed 25 Brown Pelicans
in 1 day just to draw 1. On
return, shot balls into an
alligator's head, for fun,
until it exploded.

Louisiana is The Pelican State.

Shoeless Joe was a Pelican.

Thru woods and swamp around Oakley, Louisiana,
searched 20 miles a day for specimens and game.

"The plentitude
is all we ever need," Paul
Blackburn, *The Parallel
Voyages.*

One day in autumn 1820, on the Ohio below Cincinnati, JAA
and two others shot:
30 Quail
1 Woodcock
27 Gray Squirrels

1 Barn Owl

1 Turkey Buzzard.

Audubon observed, March 1821, parties of New Orleans sportsmen and meat market hunters shooting American Golden Plovers to the tune of 48,000 kills. A man bagged 756 birds that day.

"I call birds

few

when I shoot

less than

one hundred

a day."

Kept his drawings in a tin-lined waterproof box. Watercolors.
Kept separate the art materials and guns. Took a shot at being
an artist. "The many foreshortenings unavoidable in groups
like these have been rendered attainable," he wrote in a letter,
"by means of squares of equal dimensions affixed both on my
paper and immediately behind the subjects before me." Finished a day with two Red-cockaded
Woodpeckers under his hat, one dying of the heat before Audubon reached his room; the
surviving caged bird escaped, so he drew the bird looking for insects in the unfinished walls.
Kept alive for two days' drawings. Released when the wing healed. Companion plate to the
picture of Wrens making their nest in an old brown hat.

His journey beyond Edward Hicks Peaceable Kingdom.
Audubon stabbed a man in the chest 1819 who had attacked him with a club
after a dispute about steamboat funding. John Keats wrote to his brother, bankrupted by an
Audubon steamboat confidence game: "I cannot help thinking Mr Audubon a
dishonest man…" (September 1819)

As a guest at plantations, JJA painted portraits for slave owners,
tutored in fencing   dancing   drawing   French. No table etiquette.
New Orleans, February 1821: negotiating with a model to
execute her commissioned portrait, the married painter says
he "felt like a bird that makes his escape from a string cage
filled with sweetmeats; had I met a stranger on the stairs I
would have been suspected for a thief."

"Indeed the presence of outstanding strengths presupposes
that energy needed in other areas has been channeled away
from them," Allen Shawn.

Recently sold at auction for $192,000: Audubon's
very long percussion fowling piece made from
figured maple stock, with checkered wrist, fitted
with brass butt plate and ramrod pipe, and engraved
"pineapple" style trigger guard. Smooth bore .60
caliber. Octagonal to round barrel. Brass bead front
site. Audubon sometimes fired mustard-seed shot in his gold-chased souvenir shotgun.
But his work-day instrument was a double-
barreled shotgun.

[Plays Shawn's "Growl" at piano.]

In Kentucky, he reported, the White Pelicans were
"so abundant" that he "often killed several at a shot."
With his double-barreled flintlock shotgun. Richard
Rhodes writes that "hunting was the cultural frame
out of which [Audubon's] encounter with birds
emerged…wild game was harvested…." Shooting
blindly into a cloud of a billion Passenger Pigeons,
below Louisville, in 1813; Audubon also witnessed,
at the Green River in summer 1816, a great slaughter
of Passenger Pigeons. March 24, 1900, Pike County,

Ohio: Press Clay Southwirth shot with his BB gun
one of the last known Passenger Pigeons. The boy
nicknamed his stuffed bird Button because the local
taxidermist had to use buttons for the eyes. The
name "passenger" is derived from French *passing by*.

"Probably the most terrifying sight a bird could see was the approach of John James
Audubon," Edwin Way Teale, biographer.

Audubon at Mill Grove, at a crisis point early in his art, realized that the birds in
his drawings looked dead. One day, he was —*off to the Creek and down with the first
King Fisher I met! I picked the bird up and carried it home by the bill, I sent for the Miller
and made him fetch me a piece of soft board,—when he returned he found me filing into
Sharp points pieces of my Wire, and proud to Show him the substance of my discovery,...I
pierced the body of the Fishing bird and fixed it on the board—another Wire passed above
his upper Mandible was made to hold the head in a pretty fair attitude, Smaller Skewers
fixed the feet according to my notions, and even common pins came to my assistance in
placing the legs and feet—the last Wire proved a delightful elevator to the Bird's Tail and
at Last there Stood before me the real Mankin of a Kings Fisher!* ("My Style of Drawing
Birds") That Kingfisher, Souder said he later said, marked the real beginning of his
career.

   "A sign of what was to come was A's drawing of a belted kingfisher he shot at
the Falls of Ohio in the summer of 1808...A drew the bird in simple profile—yet it
appears utterly real, from the rich blue of its fat, compact body, to its wispy head
crest and powerful, spiky beak. The eye, especially, looks *alive*...his feelings for the
first time entered his drawings in a way that imparted the most human of all traits to
his subjects: consciousness." (William Souder)

Jayland

Stunned the stunning bird sat there   shimmering head.

Claim

Audubon pretended he'd been born in Louisiana.

Plenty

Audubon's usual travel meal was bread and milk.

Audubon suffered dementia in his last years,
ringing the bell for a dozen meals a day.

Brown Pelican

STATE BIRD OF LOUISIANA

SHOOTING FLANNERY

Analyzing the appearance of a peacock as he stands with his
tail folded, I find the parts incommensurate with the whole.
—Flannery O'Connor, "The King of the Birds"

She has dressed for McTyre's visit
as if attending a funeral.
For the photoshoot, she chose:
the dark dress, a string of pearls,
low black heels and pantyhose.
He has driven down from Atlanta
the two hours to the Oconee.
Her Andalusia had been
the plantation house
for acres worked by slaves
then share-croppers.
George Wallace was gubnah.
Before he got to the house,
He could hear the screams
of the birds.
He found himself sitting
in the writer's living room
being closely chaperoned
by her self-portrait with
peacock. He needed air.
A thin slice of humidity.
So he shot her
and the two peacocks
outside: first, on red brick
steps, which looked dangerous,
then out into the driveway.
He was thinking how
the aluminum crutches

strapped to both Stalag arms

clashed nicely against

the fat birds strutting past

rustling petticoat tails.

This whole year, she will write no stories.

I am in Louisiana and this is Georgia, I have to remind myself.

The Peacock appears here in the poem, the wrong bird. Neither

fish nor songbird, loud calls, certainly nothing called for.

What do I do with you? Erase your tracks and sweep up?

Do you lead me away to whack ludicrous bushes, or

was your tail clipt

                     by rocks slammed shut?

I know the Peacock's tail

       has open eyes

when it's closed.

Cocteau's Orphee.

"The Bird sings with its fingers."

There is

some confusion even among experts.

A million radio listeners believed they heard a live performance of the duet from Dvorak's

"Songs My Mother Taught Me," on the night of May 19, 1924. Beatrice Harrison's cello

playing in the darkening woods—and a Nightingale!

Questions remain.

Can birds be said to "sing"?

Did the Nightingale sing Dvorak?

Was it a nightingale or another species?

The concert in the woods was into its third hour and the bird was a no show. We know the BBC

had hired Maude Gould (who could famously whistle *in* her throat) to stand by to whistle

the bird's part.

Respighi's bird,
scored for the Common Nightingale in "The Pines of Rome,"
might be Thrush Nightingales or Song Thrushes
(captive or in nature)
on the many recordings.

Messiaen learned,
and Trevor Hold told us,
when he slowed down field tapes of birdsongs for study,
they were not songs: what the human ear
could not catch
made the sounds
incomprehensible.

My Messiaen is more
musician
than ornithologist;
Audubon
"more artistically exciting
than authentic." (Mynott)
The yellow shirt
with bright blue parrots
is a point of unity
in her story about
the grandmother,
who "'would have been
a good woman…if it had
been somebody there
to shoot her
every minute
of her life.'"

June 27, 2022

Punk rocker Hoatzin
plays
Darwin's Tree!
for his guitar
Then burns it
on stage.

[I can read more clearly what I'd written in 2014, before Covid: *The poet of late-capitalism in his refusal to negate the negative in our e-culture, going back at least to the deaths of the last so-called heroic figures such as Olson, Duncan, Bunting, HD, Pound and Williams, is but a flightless bird, ungainly, whose long neck is still used to poke into odd places, the ostrich who swallows the watch simply because it glittered one day in his binocular eyes among an otherwise dull world. So our smartphones keep the time instead, for quotidian monsters outstripping any Ensor imagined....*

"You ruined it.

"You ruined it.

"You dropped your cellphone in the urinal, you ruined it."]

I'll show them cut second base in stride blurr off to third, I'll show them why they brot me up from Indianapolis, it will require a slide, I know I will go in headfirst and grab the bag. Safe? Umpire is pointing to the ground. Out? Is pointing to the iphone popped out my back pocket. Answer it.

…as one descends toward the south
…talents and virtues become ever rarer
among those who govern.
—Alexis de Tocqueville, *Democracy in America*

KINGFISH/ER

Some clod the truth has snatched from the ground,
and with fire has fashioned to a momentary man.
—"The Sovereignty of Ethics"

To the Public
   —inside one fugitive span, we've lived
to see
         what Kingfish missed:
"95% of the wealth controlled
              by 15% of the population"
become the 1 Per Cent.
We witness the death of modernism
From old age,
              its delirious promises
              drowned out
In the triumph of capitalism
                        without democracy.

Poetry didn't die
It woke up during surgery
To the lights the pain the doctors talking
And remembers
Everything

On his first day as president, Huey Long has Roosevelt back on his feet, like the
country, and appoints him Secretary of the Navy. (A young FDR first strode upon the
DC stage as Navy Assistant Secretary.) So the author promotes the former president
to demote him, flies backwards the Humming Bird & Wm. Grant Stills' bayou retro
opera—a black composer has Bazile choose Aurore, a spirit of the past, over Clothide.

Flannery O'Connor, at five years, taught a chicken to walk backwards. In the 1932 British Pathé newsreel, the pigeon-toed girl is identified as "Mary O'Connor of Savannah, Georgia." All the birds and animals of the farm are made to walk backwards by the filmmakers, so the documentary is ambiguous like (fast forward) the author's fiction.

A child's mind easily turns birds into dinosaurs.
Darwin quotes Audubon three times in *The Origin of Species*.
For twenty years before he wrote, the evolving beaks of Galápagos Finches sang to Darwin.

Builder Of Bridges
and hurled by hurricanes to a birdless place
the waving flags… –Ted Berrigan, Sonnet III

Order

at the rap of

the gavel;

witness

the end of days

already happened.

de Tocqueville visited Louisiana to tour the PENITENTiary.

"RESEMBLANCES" IS THIS CHYRON RUNNING BENEATH THE PAGE. IT CONTAINS KEY WORDS AND PHRASES, A LEXICON, THE POET LIFTED READING THE RICHARD WHITE BIOGRAPHY, AND

I the disenfranchised,

[Keats' steps
too low
for vision,
our poet hops
into Shelley's
car, his guide
no Rousseau
but Long.

having found the vista

at the Spanish steps

depressed,

am hustled away by Huey Long

into the sky

Or is it
stepping off
the elevator
at floor 34?]

and shown Amerika.

"I'm a small fish there in Washington.
But I am a Kingfish to the folks down in Louisiana.
Holy mackerel!"

[The Kingfish likes to exclaim

"holy mackerel!"]

THINKING OF DONALD TRUMP. UNINHIBITED…BUFFOONERY…CIRCUS-LIKE CAMPAIGN…YOU
MAY ALSO LIKE #SPAMTON…CULT FOLLOWING…DEMAGOGUE (IS "FEALTY" A KEATS WORD?)…

Kingfish is many things to many people. He is the monomaniac lawyer who dared fight the Standard Oil monopoly, the populist who taxed the rich to share the wealth, who took Bryant's motto EVERY MAN A KING finding FDR too conservative, the confidence man who put on blackface to appropriate George Stevens' catchphrase out of the mouth of the white voice actor playing Kingfish on the radio show "Amos and Andy" whose theme song was taken from J.C. Breil's orchestral score for *The Birth of a Nation* the epic silent film D.W. Griffith adapted from Thomas Dixon's novel and play *The Clansman!* The Klan loathed the Longites.

NOW, AS BEFORE in the "Parlement of Foules"

Fact has lost control—

all the birds flock home

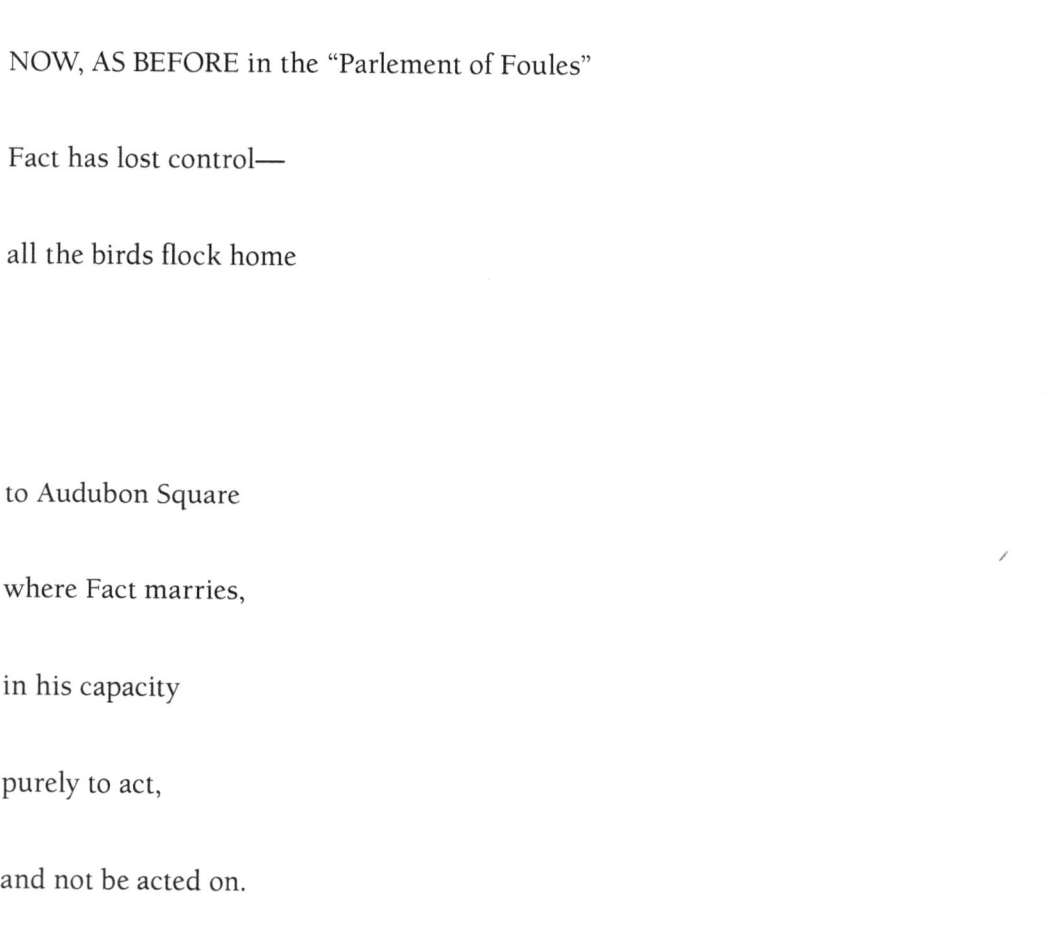

to Audubon Square

where Fact marries,

in his capacity

purely to act,

and not be acted on.

TEMPESTUOUS REIGN…DELIGHT IN SHATTERING POLITICAL TRADITIONS…BRAZEN…POLITICAL WHIM…VINDICTIVE…"HE NOT ONLY DESTROYED MANY OF HIS ENEMIES, CAME CLOSE TO

[Catsup on the wall,

mad king throttling

his driver's neck, etc.]

All petitioning couples

who come before him.

knowing death to be

a vow taken seriously.

for Assassination is

the formal marriage,

publicly declared

before mankind and

until the end of record,

between the victim

and the assassin,

whose names

shall henceforth

Colliers, Dec. 1930
describes him being
"ruthless as a machine
gun." *Colliers* in June
1933, "his eyes—soft,

protruding robin's
eggs—are nevertheless
bold." Kingfish quotes
both Walter Davenport
articles in parallel
columns for *EMAK*.

"Like Orpheus, all the poets
felt violent death staring them
in the face. Everywhere,
publishers had been pillaged
and collections of verse
burnt," Apollinaire's
The Poet Assassinated.

be one.

Dissolution of marriage,

by neglect separation divorce decree

citing irreconcilable differences,

is impossible.

Some marriages:

John Kennedy and Lee Harvey Oswald

Robert Kennedy and Sirhan Sirhan

Martin Luther King and James Earl Ray

Malcom X and many

John Lennon and Mark David Chapman

George Moscone and Dan White

Harvey Milk and Dan White

Emmett Till and Roy Bryant

DESTROYING REPUBLICAN RULE"...DIVISIVE: EXPLOIT THE WEAKNESSES AND FEARS OF THE
PEOPLE; FEAR AND EMPLOYMENT; EMPLOY DEMOCRATIC MEANS TO ACHIEVE UNDEMOCRATIC

Emmett Till and J.W. Milan

Mahatma Gandhi and Nathuram Vinayak Godse

Leon Trosky and Ramón Mercader

Tograth and Croniamantal

Archduke Ferdinand and Gavrilo Princip

William McKinley and Leon Czolgosz

Stanford White and Harry Kendall Thaw

James Garfield and Charles Guiteau

Abraham Lincoln and John Wilkes Booth

Joseph Smith and many

Jean-Paul Marat and Charlotte Corday

Huey Long and Dr. Carl Weis

Long opens his campaign autobiography by invoking Cellini.

The libretto of Kingfish and the kingfisher in the Senate chamber abandoned like school's out. The only sound possible is the uncaptivating moby-dick filibuster; the feathered

ENDS...ORCHESTRATED ELECTIONS...DURING ELECTION KIDNAPPED THOSE WHO ACCUSED HIM OF ADULTEROUS AFFAIRS..."DRAIN THE SWAMPS!"—46 PER CENT OF AMERICA'S WETLANDS ARE

maximus is being held captive there. Ahab Kingfish drones on beyond 15 hours straight: reads selections from the bible from Shakespeare the Constitution and the snakes of Loozyana stories about his drunk uncle quotations by Hugo a biographical sketch of Frederick the Great shares his special recipe for salad dressing how to fry oysters—did he read into the record the five cantos of "Evangeline"?—takes up 59 pages in the Congressional Record, or about the size of a small book of poems, all the while stoking glasses of milk and handfuls of chocolate to keep his energy up. For this passage, the players keep time individually. Claude Pepper wouldn't arrive in the Senate for months after Long left; and Charles Olson chimes in a decade afterwards. Eric Dolphy, for his part, is making mallard sounds and time seems malleable again. Circular.

Everybody writes about Kingfish's filibuster
few read the text.
Why Pound, waiting for the mail, quotes John Adams at length: the whole text of his filibuster or settling for the form of one? To read the Kingfish,

typed in key words "Victor Hugo." Find   The invitation was a
Hugo's story of parliament ("I skip a little—,"   kind of filibuster, like
Kingfish says at one point. When Sen. Clark   Strom Thurmon's,
challenges him, "Of what edition?" he replies: to the boy. He wants
"The de luxe edition." Has his storied uncle   to go home but the
tell a bartender: "I am going to stay here   choir was singing
with you until you find out how to mix drinks   ALL THE VERSES
people like."—a warning to the weary senators.   of each hymn, giving
There's the chicken-coup case. His reviews of   the sinners in the
Articles I and II of the Constitution. "Let me   room plenty of time
alone." A third recipe is for Roquefort cheese   to confess.
salad dressing. Where are him reading aloud
the five cantos of "Evangeline"? Did I only imagine a brief history of Audubon on
the Mississippi? The banks of the river are too slick   with bird shit   to walk.

IN LOUISIANA. THE STATE'S DWINDLING BAYOUS SWAMPS MARKS THE DECLINE IN FOOD HARVESTS OF SHRIMP OYSTERS BLUE CRABS… ASSAULTS ON "THE LYING PRESS"…

"I have shown you this

so you will know

it's all happened before,

your days are not

unprecedented,

democracy will muddle by

as democracy does

killing time

to fill the end of days:

less in the package

but we are happy

just to get it.

In Fact,

I am judge and jury.

"I can make those
voting machines sing
'Home Sweet Home.'"
—Earl K. Long, brother

CRONYISM: PACKED THE COURTS AND THE BUREAUCRACY WITH LOYALTISTS…HUEY LONG
EMPLOYED HIS OWN POLL WORKERS: HIS MAN C.S. BARNES DOCTORED VOTING RECORDS

To be sure, votes

don't count themselves."

"It was Long's custom to call an extra session of the legislature whenever the occasion arose where certain laws were necessary to protect him or to provide ways and means of achieving some political or personal end. This custom continued after he went to the U.S. Senate, he using the Governor Allen for whatever purpose he had in mind. On the night of September 8, 1935, (Sunday) one of such extra sessions was being held, the fifth or sixth such session in 1935." (Inspector's Report to Mutual Life Insurance Co., Nov. 9, 1936)

The DeSoto Literary Conference

BALBOA: You've swapped your birds. You won't find the Nightingale in America—she's European. People in a hurry mistake her, people who read too fast. Smartass poets make us feel slow. What you are hearing in Louisiana, if you bother traveling to sites, sounds to me like our Mocking Bird. Here, I looked it up for you:

But where is that favored land?...It is, reader, in Louisiana that these bounties of nature are in the greatest perfection. It is there that you should listen to the love-song of the Mocking Bird, as I at this moment do. That's John James Audubon's "Ornithological Biography," nevermind Messiaen's Catalogue. *See how he flies round his mate, with motions as light as those of the butterfly! His tail is widely expanded, he mounts in the air to a small distance, describes a circle, and, again alighting, approaches his beloved one, his eyes gleaming with delight...His beautiful wings are gently raised, he bows to his love, and again bouncing upwards, opens his bill, and POURS FORTH HIS MELODY, FULL OF EXULTATION AT THE CONQUEST WHICH HE HAS MADE.*

Well, you really didn't know all you need to know to write competently, did you, Cortez. Now that you know, will you abandon your poem? You seem better equipped to mock your sources, especially when it comes to birds. Amateur. You come in here like the duck bearing leeks! What IS the nature of nature in poetry? And WHY in the name drag in poor Huey Long? Better off rewriting fish for bird. Ah, the current could be sky or stream!

...WRITES HIS OWN CAMPAIGN BOOK, "MY FIRST DAYS IN THE WHITE HOUSE"...SURVIVED MULTIPLE IMPEACHMENTS...TRUTH WAS IMMATERIAL—TOLD A CATHOLIC AUDIENCE

A simile

is not much

to go on.

And get this straight: Shawn's "Song of the Tango" is no birdsong—it is a mating dance.
Where's the like of Audubon's alight/delight in your poem? You don't understand we love
Long who seduced us. Wait, there's more: *The musical powers of this bird have often been
taken notice of by European naturalists…Some of these persons have described the notes of the
Nightingale as occasionally fully equal to those of our bird. I have frequently heard both species
in confinement, and in the wild state, and without prejudice, have no hesitation in pronouncing the
notes of the European Philomel equal to those of a soubrette of taste, which, could she study under
a MOZART, might perhaps become very interesting in her way. But to compare her essays to the
finished talent of the Mocking Bird, is, in my opinion, quite absurd.*

[Note: Johnson lists eight published score titles from 1953 to 1975 that name birds in
English, in which Messiaen identifies the Nightingale.]

CORTEZ: Esteemed Dr. B.,

How OCD of me.—

I thot you said "smile"

and had to look twice.

About the simile,

you may be right.

"I do not seek a synthesis

but a melee."

I have your recitation on Huey's animal attraction. The poem enlarges, thanks to you. I
am fishing for Kingfish, my line in the water in the shadow of his bridge in the fissiparous
Mississippi birdscape. My legs and feet and are soaked. I am all in.

HE WAS CATHOLIC, A PROTESTANT AUDIENCE HE WAS BAPTIST…EMERGED FROM NORTHERN
LOUISIANA'S BIBLE BELT…KINGFISH SPOKE WITHOUT NOTES…1930 PROMISES ECONOMIC

You dive-bomb me as if I am Mocking Bird's enemy. But I have already uncovered the truth of what you see in his resemblance to Turdus polyglottys ("many-tongued mimic")! Candidate Long at the podium leaping into the air and fluttering down. Filibustering Long singing all day and night. Huey P. Long was a mocker in many voices:

Cajun

seductive

comedian

radio Kingfish

poor farmer

country folk

hooveroosevelt

huckster

voice of the people

lawyer before the Supreme Court

drum major for the LSU marching band

Baptist evangelist

ur-Foghorn Leghorn.

Minutes (how to catch Kingfish)

Your chances of catching Kingfish are better if you employ more than one rod at a time.

Kingfish have good eyesight and can detect metal leaders underwater.

Use live baitfish that are at least six inches long.

If the bait is backward on the hook, Kingfish may not strike.

Kingfish can strike your bait at up to fifty miles per hour.

Be ready to grab Kingfish by the tail when he gets close.

GROWTH WILL BE ALMOST MAGIC"; COMPARE TRUMP'S COVID WILL ONE DAY DISAPPEAR LIKE MAGIC…PRANKS ON SENATE FLOOR—STAGED 5 FILIBUSTERRS AGAINST ROOSEVELT'S

Thirties Pop Songs

"Listening to a lyrebird sing may be like listening to a very old tape."

A woman as if by Murnane hears a resemblance between the Flute

Lyrebird's song and two popular songs. "It was on Allanbank," Australia, 1936,

"I first heard the lyrebird mimicking the flute. It gave wonderful flute imitations

of the 'Mosquito Dance,' 'The Keel Row,' and the scales…

One of the neighbors had a lyrebird in captivity," Martha Manns recalled for Norman

Robinson, in 1973. "The man played the flute, and the lyrebird learnt to mimic

the sounds. Later, he released the bird, and then the other lyrebirds also picked

up the sounds…

"Fragments of the flute player's music were passed down by generations of

lyrebirds."

"…Australia was the home of the most ancient songbirds…." (*The Largest Arian Radiation*)

"Songbirds of the same species don't all sing the same song. Geographically isolated

populations often develop distinct vocal repertories…Songbirds learn their songs rather

than inherit them. They make an innate array of sounds, but young birds learn to sing by

listening to the older birds around them. Youngsters spend their first winter dreaming about

those songs (literally: studies have found that they 'practice' in their sleep). In the spring

they begin to sing them aloud." (*Nature Anatomy*)

Robinson: "…Martha Manns told me that in the middle of the night…she heard

a flute player playing a tune, and she rushed out…and the flute player was 60

feet up in a tree…"

"BLUE BUZZARD"…NICKNAMED ENEMIES AFTER ANIMALS…REFUSED TO RESIGN GOV'SHIP
WHILE SERVING IN SENATE…NAMED KINGFISH IN SENATE…COULDN'T STAND BEING TOUCHED.

The Swamp Foxes Play Ball

He took the call

"This is the Governor speaking."

Evangelist Francis Marion Tarwater established a four-year college

with a basketball team seven scholarships and a nickname,

paid no taxes, and was appointed by Kingfish to fill out a term

as Justice in another successful move to pack the highest court.

It was the governor speaking,

"Got a hole for you to fill, son."

Moonshine

"Look on my Works, ye Mighty, and despair!"

Over 9,700 miles of new roads,

more than 100 bridges

         (shaking the people's hands),

and how many tons

over the years

of bird shit?

    And who cleans up?

Who power-sprays away the patina from the statue

of the great man,

        builder of roads and bridges,

        man with a hole in his sock

man of the people cast in bronze

admiring how far he's come: the Art Deco tower

constructed on his word?

Man for the birds.

(High up on the south side
of the Cathedral of Learning
nest the Peregrine Falcons.
Pittsburghers watch via cam
to see if Hope kills her chicks.
Fern Hollow bridge goes to Tree of Life.)
The new state capital on a bank of the Mississippi.
Replete   with freezes and, at the grand
entrance, carvings of Audubon   Charles-Étienne
      Gayarré*   and Kingfish.
An immigrant holding a Ph.D.
back in his country meanwhile
hums while he scrubs "Three
Little Birds."

*Confederate planter (his plantation is Audubon Park), conspiratory theorist and
multi-volume historian of the state, a Know Nothing.

RESEMBLANCES, 1-27

To Allen Shawn

1 The Arrangement

Three etudes

first,

then six more

makes a book.

Messiaen uses the term "book" in *Catalogue d'Oiseaux*.

Later came two

books of nine,

with "hints of

Messiaen in

books two

and three."

Allen Shawn's Etudes for Piano started as a set of three.

Don't be so surprised to come across Messiaen—Audubon—Keats and O'Connor here on our Green Mountain hike. On Rendezvous Peak, I look up from drinking glacier melt from my hands—to meet a couple from my hometown in Ohio! Another time, taking in Yellowstone Lake, I bumped into my dean! Frees me to cast Audubon as Roberto in *Down By Law,* turn around and direct Jean Lanier in the Audubon biopic. (However, I would not mess with the perfect short films of *The Audubon Trilogy.*) Ask any stranger to snap our picture. A big

smile.

Just now Mathilda tells me she had submitted in Allen's class a short story picturing Messiaen and Loriod on a day recording more birdsongs, and I immediately want the story for a kind of preface to remember my poem by.

2 My Written Assignment on Messiaen's Quartet Begins With Four, and Is Late

Begin with four birds in a prose cage.
Study the laws of their captivity songs
being careful to set them free
before the world ends again.

Do not expect help, much less understanding.
It broke your heart when they flew away.
Learn that it is the nature of birds
to return to their cage thru the open door.

So why four novels?

3 Dear Irby

Those eggs in the catalpa hatched, Ken,
everybody survived. The parents are
busy as hell. Thot you'd like to know.
Please tell Gerrit for me. Love, Rich

4

The overnight storm that toasted my computer
returned my daughter's lost necklace.
The birds have woven the velvet string
into their mud nest, for stability.

5 Keats' feet

There is no one song but all songbirds share

the structure of their syrinx and the ability

to learn new songs; many songbirds have

the "perching foot":

three forward-pointing toes

and a backwards toe, or hallux, articulated

by separate tendons. (Ben Crair)

6 I ask for a lead

not to take one, just listening, thanks.

doing a little detective work like my hero Bolaño,

footnoting a few well-known affinities

besides I didn't bring my music. So I improvise,

ask A if he's heard Martha Manns' story. I don't read

music just listening. Long ago, the pigeons of Venice

pecked out my eyes.

Writes back to me his Piano Etudes may "evoke Messiaen's sound world and vocabulary."

And recommends "Song of the Tango-Bird," tho not birdsong, as a dialog with "Merle Noir."

I track it down. Sure enuf, tho I hadn't detected it before—the forensic boys turn up

Messiaen's DNA on the flute and the piano. The mystery remains how could anyone but a bird

get himself out of that room?

7 A bird is first a pie.

Messiaen's signature is uncial ("letters") like a tree trunk and not, as we might suppose, cursive ("running away") like the little birds.

8

"It is the contrapuntal music of Bach that [Schoenberg, in *Style and Idea*] described as producing its material not by development but 'by a procedure rather to be called unraveling,'…though written 'in one single line, yet furnishes various sounds.'" (Allen Shawn, *Arnold Schoenberg's Journey*) As I, the poet, quote A.S. quoting Schoenberg on Bach—my new poem breaks

into song!

or at least

Sprechstimme.

9 John Francis

Who else would say

"Southern-fried grackle,"

and meant it?

Preachy Edward Hicks needs to include birds in the Kingdoms

so I can hear him.

10 Wittgenstein be damned

I have

a pain

in my notebook.

(Exposure to loud) music (during adolescence and young adulthood) can lead to (hearing) problems later in life.

11 Loud

A wardrobe of white linen suits by Godchaux of New Orleans

But neck ties

all colors of screaming birds.

12 The Parallel Voyages

Landing can be big as a barn,

or nest-tight

Coming in, after

the Cranes

Stephen & Hart.

Or small as a postage stamp in the ocean

like Cage,

or Mahler, late of the near star.

Paul Blackburn's favorite bird was the Wood Thrush.

Morning after landing at MSY, among the many amenities

at The Degas House: the Creole Breakfast

comes with mimosas and bloody mary.

The Big Easy night never cools down,

so the days are insufferable   an endless line of relatives

to be painted, such dull

portraits of the new world

Degas has painted himself wrapped in cotton   hiding

beneath a French-language newspaper.

The only one unfazed by humidity is Billie Holiday.

13

Dr, Weiss was shot
sixty-one times in
six seconds.
Justice Fourner,
an eyewitness,
remembered Long
when he was shot
made "a hoot."

14 To the Legislators on Legislating

"It is somewhat like hog-killing time;
everybody is called in to something
as though it were the gathering of
the hounds for a great chase."
(*Congressional Record*)

15 Pride

Kingfish launched his campaign for governor
in St. Martinsville, at the Evangeline Oak
beside the Bayou Teche.
The speechmaker makes it sound
as if the poem were Louisiana history.
"And it is here under this oak where..." and
"Your tears in this country, around this oak,
have lasted for generations."

In the Long fellow story
of Acadian exile
and the birth of proud Cajun,
Labiche and Arceneaux,
only resemble the lovers
Evangeline and Gabriel.
The area is a bird habitat today.

16 For Dessie

Pore country folk
walked or rowed
to Baton Rouge
some rode
the backs of farm animals
to peer into the coffin
at the body
of the man
who built the hardtop roads.

I never heard you called Dessie.
I still hear the sounds of Kennedy haters in the church
old-time tent meeting sounds from the evangelist who pounds
the pulpit like Bryant
sounds recalled by Kingfish
at St. Martinsville.
Shall we gather at the river?

neat pews
broken teeth like headstones line mouths that spew
the unburied hymnals
song we sang most Sundays

of Robert Lowry in Brooklyn
meditating on the Revelation
already familiar from Hollywood western soundtracks.

Yes, we'll gather at the river,
The beautiful, beautiful river;
Gather with the saints at the river
That flows by the throne of God.

17

Kingfish strolls by a bald cypress dating back to Audubon.
The live oaks wear robes of Spanish moss.
Dwarf palmettos genuflect on either side.
On the list of the protected birds of Louisiana are
songbirds, Falcons, and Kingfishers.
We stand by a bald cypress dating back to Kingfish.

18 CAPTCHA

Kingfish tacked 26,000,000 handbills, 1,000 to 1,800 words, to trees telephone poles barns. The one I
saw was 11 x 21 inches, from 1934, a call to organize your own Share Our Wealth chapter.
Before I left the archives, I also visited a 1968 billboard from Vermont.

19 The View from the Stop

LOUISIANA THE PELICAN STATE State Capital Bldg., Baton Rouge, La. & LOUISIANA'S
TWO GREATEST MONUMENTS Conceived and Built By the Late U.S. Senator: State
Capital, Baton Rouge & New Huey P. Long Bridge, New Orleans (his portrait inserted).

Two vintage linen

postcards from Kansas

arrived today wrapped

in a newspaper

article on Reds.

20

Kingfish designed the new governor's mansion to resemble the White House.

21

Had he lived, Kingfish's voice might have sounded like oldpennwarren Reading Aloud for the camera.
Impossible that Billie Holiday sings with Armstrong in the movie *New Orleans*.

22 The Raggedy 9

They'd booed him

all day.

So next time up,

he doffed his cap

releasing—a Sparrow

into the laughing air.

HIPOPALORUM!

LOPOPAHIRUM!

23 The SABR Mechanics

The press photograph of Huey Long and Ava Bradley, suited up in Cleveland uniforms (except for street shoes), shaking hands. They are smiling. It is spring training in 1935. The governor

and the owner mock the baseball players who wear spikes. In the midsummer heat of his sermon, Billy Sunday would slide across the stage—Safe! at Home, with God.

24 Tweet

Deadly bird flu has been reported
in mallard ducklings at the Reflecting
Pool in the Mall. Officials warn
that droppings on sidewalks around
the Lincoln Memorial could pose
a danger to DC tourists.

============================

Please tear along the line and return.

25

The massive crowd for Dr. Weiss
Resembled Huey's turnout.
A Kinglet weighs about two pennies.
Ravens are the largest songbirds in the world.

26 Lots of theories, a few details

Dour doubter, double

tour the marble hall

to your heart's content

Dip your digits for yourself

Into every bullet hole

The miracle is not there

Kingfish absorbed it

And he has lit out

Absconded

With the evidence.

At rest, it resembles

Nothing so much as

A penny the kids let

The train flatten,

The souvenir slug.

27 Down Home

Down home,

The birds have quit singing,

Or else the rain drowns them

Out, and all I need to know.

The cats are cowering

In place at the door to

The stairs. Time for

Lighting the lights

For finding the one

Good candle. We're in

For a big one.

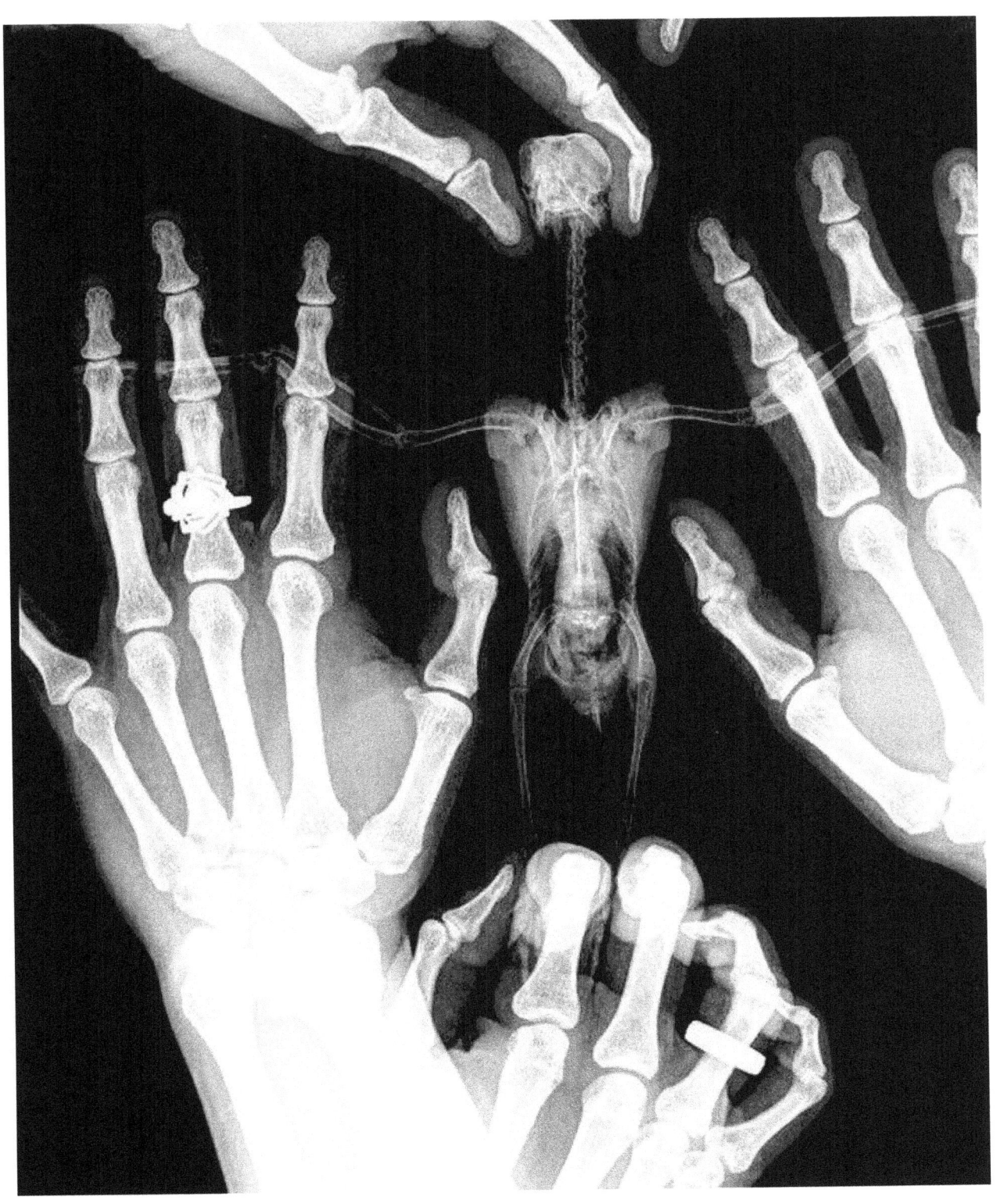

The trouble with war for a botanist—
he daren't drop out of the line of march
to examine a flower. What flower?
Shell-burst—observe a sky-exotic
attract a bomber-bird?
—Lorine Niedecker, draft for unpublished poem

GOING TO THE SOURCE

For Heather Woods

You can see how we return to our source.
And there is never any death.
—Lorine Niedecker to her husband on a car trip

Let 'er fffly!

Her letters fly to Eshelman like airmail from the typer in perfect V formation turning her head to admire the migrating flock beyond her doing.

"…I figured after 40 years of more or less precise writing I cd. afford to let go…close your eyes and let the music carry you."

And the letter to Corman:
"W.H. Hudson says birds feel something akin to pain (and fear) just before migration and nothing alleviates the feeling except flight…I must be going to migrate."

"It's a feeling of the vertical more than the simple straight line." Open.

At the end, "…the battle with myself as to the new form I feel but don't quite dare use." She could only read natural history during "my strange winter" did manage "PAEAN TO PLACE" good enough for the state historical marker her cabin flooded so many times, she reopened it so often, only the essential things remained inside. Or what you can put in a rowboat at the last minute. The few odd things that were my mother's are safe in me.

Try scraping with a letter opener the river mud from Morrison carpets.

Sculptures of birds wrought from iron too heavy to scatter at her approach. One feather must weigh as much as the Buick.

Febrile, she wakes at night, her husband works third shift, to write down "A stone holding down the stack of pages."

She is stopped just there
                              unable to go up, or down,
          marbles spilled across marble stairs.

Song sinks

like a pebble
thrown in
for luck.
The exception being Gail Roub's painting
                    the warbler singing yellow green
                                        for St. Francis. But even then the prothonotary
stop.

Bertholf would be assassinated in her name by lawyers who maintain still a cage with the door removed.

Gingham, "dyed in the yarn."

The woman in the gingham dress writes to Roub after "Wintergreen Ridge": "Much taken up with how to define a way of writing which is not Imagism *nor Objectivism fundamentally* nor Surrealism alone...I loosely called it 'reflections.'

"I used to feel that I was goofing off unless I held only to the hard image, but now I do this reflection";

whose work began in Surrealism

"Travel, said he of the broken umbrella, enervates
The point of stop…" (*Poetry*, 1933),

and stopped with Objectivism

"Stops?
Even for death" ("LZ")

The woman in the gingham dress awaiting his judgments.

The time she eventually had to stop
"In the transcendence
of convalescence
the translation
of Basho."

"Basho's // backwater"
            frustrated, so she wrote
            IN EXCHANGE FOR HAIKU,
and didn't stop till she arrived at "Wintergreen Ridge," at the end of the mapped, researched
world. Frustrated her poems cannot add up
to Basho's long journey. Realizing that
Basho had many huts and none—
imagine a stopping place among all possible stops—
her land was prone to flooding.

                "I was the solitary plover / a pencil / for a wing-bone."

The piping plover does not sing, she squeaks.
("Seven years the one
dress

for town once a week

One for home

    faded blue-striped

as she piped

her cry");

the piping bird is not seen to stop to rest

(note her short quick step even in her sixties).

The piping bird runs beside the flooded field

Does not design a nest

sits eggs instead

in a dimple

in the sand

("What would they say if they knew

I sit for two months on six lines

of poetry.")

If the woman in the gingham dress migrates, she only "Throw[s] things / to the flood."

We have a list of Basho's

earthly possessions,

and maybe Susan Tichy's *Field Guide.*

Even the car trips were governed

by look no further.

Stops like a caesura in music notation

and lots of stops

not just anywhere

between lines.

LN: "What maddens me on all automobile trips: you're traveling that way because it's easier to *stop* whenever you want to, but you can't stop, not just anywhere…you have to keep going, actually it's one of the rules of the road." Her husband Al, the driver, would have layed down the rules of the road—

Zukofsky was always the only driver, the life heavily redacted black as eyebrows as rubber tires.

—to see the flowers and rocks whizzing past, she notes, "you'd have to walk—someday."

"The pebble has traveled."

The woman in the gingham dress was driven to write poems.

Driven to write poems, she was always looking for signs.

A: "Yes, well, help me read the road signs, they're so small in Canada—
and greenish, they melt into the forests."
L: "What signs?"

"At one place, almost hidden in the trees a sign: Post Office, and it pointed into the forest!"

She waited till
After the wedding,
To tell Al she was a
poet
"A what?"

"Can knowledge be conveyed that isn't felt?
But if transport's the problem—"

"…the sign said LOOSE SAND into which the car got stuck. I ran to the shore…"

Restless like the plover running back and forth between two points, from "Ah your face / but
it's whether / you can keep me warm" and "Beauty: impurities in the rock."

The reader has arrived at the point in her poem when the nerdy wing glasses are exchanged for
sunglasses and Al's binoculars.

Being careful never to exceed the posted speed limits in geological time.

The Great Lakes she is witnessing will be tropical, and the skeletons of ore ships exposed. In the Flood of '59, she had to row to her house. The rock formations survive above or below water. Her cabin is elevated from the floods on a foundation of concrete blocks; on road trips, the small woman in the gingham dress perched on pillows to see out of the car. When he thought she wasn't looking, he thinks, my wife seems fretful of things beyond my ken, he had no words for it, a thing beyond a cabin and the threat of flooding. Gulls on the parking lot meant a storm on the lake. The husband prided himself on fixing things. To fix a clock wound up too tight you'd first have to open it. Put the wife's copy of *Leaves of Grass* to practical use, smoothing a wrinkled dollar.

After a week, she carried home
only postcards, park pamphlets,
and a single agate
Buried her wish for the longpoem
beneath feather illusions airless rock.

"…history books are just a more wordy sort of travel brochure," Murnane.

The Driver

For heaven's sake though see to the driver!
—William Carlos Williams

"I'm safer in a car than I am on foot."
The driver is missing his right hand at the wrist, suffered
a printing press accident as a young man,
but the stump helps
steady the car
on the north-country roads.
A man only needs one good hand
to paint a house, fish, drink, and wipe
his own ass. The 1962 deluxe tan
came with push-button windows. (She may have agreed with family:
"They've bought a
hummingbird—
you can't haul
anything in it.")
Al still works
third shift
at Ladish Drop Forge,
Packer Avenue, and
sleeps days.
The unreality of the world felt by the 11-to-7 worker
is not the same unreality the poet wife feels.
The husband reads at the dinner table;
his new wife, "thin for thought," writes
"Away from the table: I eat books,"
although he has never read the poem.
"We voted," she wrote of their union,
"both going / into the one booth,"
hubby "must have thought /
it was a hunting / blind."

Al slept through Jonathan Williams come to lunch

in the next room.

"I'm better off than most." Frank

Fithen the armless freak drove himself to the circus.

Judge Corley. Even Roosevelt

was known to drive a car.

Unlike those guys, I don't require hardware. I grab

the spinner knob, and drive like a champ.

He has long ago stopped missing his hand.

Nearing retirement, the man appeared to cover long expanses of highway with the flair of a

sport handling his like-new Buick, his sixtyish wife holding down the far end of the bench

seat made only a distracted navigator. In short,

she was not a driver so her map-reading in situ

was malaprop for the sudden urgencies of a moving car.

She had done months of research for the trip in local libraries

and planned a poem in her head. It would be her breakthrough—

a poem as long and clear as a stretch of Great Lakes geology.

Her previous pieces were hard as polished agate.

Rock inside rock:

The and A

before nouns.

Zukofsky's letter asks her, after Duns Scotus, is it really "Impossible for matter to think"?

Lush Source

Let me walk you thru it.

Looking back,
it was the extinct carrier pigeon led me
to travel to some of the spots on Niedecker's map
and visit the source of the Mississippi, her later poetry,
and my subsequent poem. I drove in researched ignorance
up river, from St. Louis, writing the poem by intuition
into the journal open on the passenger seat, as I went.
I traveled light, with a tourist's empty head and lugging
around in my backpack the new Humphrey Carpenter Pound
to open on my bed and read myself to sleep wherever I was.

"Scent of slab wood
heat from my stove
the sleepy taste
layers of comforters
pillows for my head
on the bed you have
made for me makes
a female appeal
to drive into and thru
still I am up driven
the idea of the poem is a source of irritation, a life beneath host skin
insomniac with a flashlight
reading outhouse walls rush
light prose. Too nervous to
read biographies I've brot.
A tick on the prick."

Only recently, thirty-two years after writing those lines of "Going to the Source," have I come to recognize

something of what I missed out on

seeing

on the trip to visit Sherman Paul, the living source of my inspiration   Ideal Reader   at Wolf Lake.

> "I'm sorry to have missed
>   Sand Lake
> My dear one tells me
>   we did not
> We watched a gopher there" (LN)

Now that I am the artist "Between the Clock and the Bed"
Suddenly five years older than LN lived to be,
Alive fifty-two years after her death.

It seems

an extinct pigeon brings me here from Audubon in my poem. Among the lines Aldo Leopold (a name I got from Sherman) wrote in "On a Monument to a Pigeon," an essay for the dedication of the Passenger Pigeon Monument at Wyalusing State Park in Wisconsin, is the clause

> "Men still live who, in their youth, remember pigeons…"

Sherman had pointed out, in a 1988 essay later gathered into *For Love of the World*, "Frederick Jackson Turner…returned to Madison in the year Leopold arrived and lived nearby on the same street and was equally present in his thought." Learning to read the land.

That trip,

I passed on the Pigeon Monument…Sherman Paul and I never mentioned Lorine Niedecker's poetry, which I hadn't thought to reread before setting out…I see I even skipped her Schoolcraft for the most part (one reference), off course, of course, turning over a few rocks. "Almost all of Leopold's philosophic and literary writings," Paul writes, "required revision." Finally, the nature writer was not "a natural writer" but had to "traveled a long way" to find his maturity. Sherman Paul's diary-entry essays, road testing what he has just read, still seem the perfect form for criticism. When I finished "Going to the Source," I had the distinct feeling it was my most open, and held that judgment over some years.

I see

all that driving to collections was a young man practicing for living alone. The sedentary life as sediment. She comes in here, 2022, in my figuring what to say for a review of Heather Woods' *Bundling*, where I hear Niedecker, although she is never quoted or used as a model for new writing, as if Heather is being dictated the long open masterpiece Neidecker left unwritten at her death. Unbidden spirits speak through the younger poet, more *Odyssey* Book XI than Yeats, folks.

So,

Woods made the sign I was awaiting not expecting (in a state of silent calling Murnane best accounts for)

for me

to begin to write a new poem, hopefully a long one, where I thought I had ended and given up to age.

The world around me, once more, was charged—I was in danger of losing my equilibrium as when

traveling and felt I had to write frantically to catch up.

But

where was this taking me—was it back to the Niedecker I'd dodged?—Certainly

away

from the end—happily reading Gerald Murnane for the first time, losing myself on the continent where

references go to die, leaving things in the open. His insistence on rereading his books kept me up nights like the old days of taking notes on a new project for the morning's work.

All
Because I'd thought of Niedecker and mentioned reading Murnane in my brief review
for
Heather.

I stop this poem OPEN

tho making Murnane a reference

Bring forward a stanza I wrote once
for Sherman to read first:

"Nature is that in which no thing can be lost
does not mean we come here, to Itasca, to find
things or those who are gone or especially ourselves;
for the transformations of Nature are inhuman.
Even in the canoe, time pulled against us downstream.
But having climbed this far above the river, I had hopes
my poem would open up to democratic vistas;
whereas I found at the top I could not bring myself
to drink the cold beer, drinking in the scale,
you had to port the bottle down the bluff.
The first mile runs north
upside down, facing Hudson Bay, ignorant of downriver reputation
below it the long backwards fall to Hannibal and below
at this stage loved by immediate family only
its life is not much longer than our own lives.
Antipodal Alberti was unaware,
upside down as he was in Mississippi history,
of mound-building culture.
Pelegrin, Dante's word for 'pilgrim.'
What bird was it our canoe started from the wild rice?

But also *peregrine* the falcon.
'Have you noticed,' she sd, 'only men
    know the names of the stars?'
She who knows every bird, mushroom,
    the sources of flint by name." (May-June 1990)

"My life / by water"

rounded pebble writ by water

"I awoke the next morning to twitterings…mixed with a marsh hush that I must have known soon after I'd known life in this world. The river had risen in the back land to within six feet of the house. Here in the lush wash, you go back to the exuberant source and start over."
("The Evening's Automobiles")

"Waded, watched, warbled"

Here is tip top kids hop across
the Mississippi
The earth turns away
One flopped on wet rock
and didn't stop
Fell the proverbial drop
of water for ninety days
the entire length of the
river till Huey's bridge
hung her up.
The water turns
bottled water bright
to muddy brown
Demonstrating all poetics is
local after all.
At times, the land seemed
to her to vaporize. Rode
a considerable distance
inside a fish. Davenport,
the rain became
a vertical flood plain.
Memphis child took her
home overnight in a jar.
Boat bottoms passed like clouds
overhead or the shadows of clouds.
"How swell of you to turn out
to greet me like this, dear reader
of poetry, with that tear
in your duct."

"She always sounded," past sixty,
"like a 12-year-old girl, a small
birdlike voice, maybe a sparrow."

(Bob Nero)

Schoolmates
called her
Squeaky.

Settle on
the object
A drop
of water.

Page with two stops.

RE/SOURCES

Barry Ahearn, *Zukofsky's "A": An Introduction*. 1983.

Amy Alznauer, *The Strange Birds of Flannery O'Connor: A Life*. Children's book illustrated by Ping Zhu. 2020.

The Original Water-Color Paintings by John James Audubon for "The Birds of America." 1966.

John James Audubon, Writings and Drawings. Library of America. 1999.

Harrison Birtwistle, *Nine Settings of Lorine Niedecker for Soprano and Cello*. Sanctuary Classics CD, 2001.

Ken Burns, *Huey Long*. DVD, 1985.

Ada Calhoun, *Also A Poet*. 2022.

Congressional Record, May 24-June 13, 1935: vol. 79.

Ben Crair, "Old World Warblers," *LRB*, 9 June 2022.

Ornette Coleman, *Skies of America*. Columbia LP, 1972.

Hermann Deutsch, *The Huey Long Murder Case*. 1963.

Robert Duncan, *Selected Poems*, ed. Robert J. Bertholf. 1993.

—————, "Pages from a Notebook," in *The New American Poetry*, ed. Donald Allen, 1960.

Ralph Waldo Emerson, "The Sovereignty of Ethics." EmersonCentral ebook. 2019.

Jon Fjeldsà, Les Christidis, and Per G.P. Ericson, *The Largest Avian Radiation: The Evolution of Perching Birds, Or the Order Passeriformes*. 2020.

Keats's Poetry and Prose, ed. Jeffrey N. Cox. 2009.

Gary Giddens, *Visions of Jazz*. 1998.

Robert Sherlaw Johnson, *Messiaen*. 1975.

David Kraft, *Birdsongs in the Music of Olivier Messiaen*. 2013.

Peter Hill and Nigel Simeon, *Messiaen*. 2005.

Huey P. Long, *Every Man A King*. 1961.

—————, *My First Days in the White House*. 1935.

Olivier Messiaen, *Catalogue d'oiseaux/Petites esquisses d'oiseaux*. Naxos CD, 1996.

—————, Cadenza for "Concert à quatre," on *Messiaen: Concert à Quatre*. Deutsche Grammophon, 1995.

—————, *Quartet for the End of Time*. EMI CD, 2008.

—————, *Turangalîla Symphonie*. Deutsche Grammophon CD, 1991.

Gerald Murnane, "First Love," in *Stream System*. 2018.

—————*Last Letter to a Reader*. 2021.

Jeremy Mynott, *Birdscapes: Birds in Our Imagination and Experience*. 2009.

Lorine Niedecker, *Collected Works*, ed. Jenny Penberthy. 2002.

Lorine Niedecker: Woman and Poet, ed. Jenny Penberthy. 1996.

Flannery O'Connor, *Mystery & Manners: Occasional Prose.* 1969.

Sherman Paul, *For Love of the World.* 1992.

Margot Peters, *Lorine Niedecker: A Poet's Life.* 2011.

Radical Vernacular: Lorine Niedecker and the Poetics of Place, ed. Elizabeth Willis. 2008.

Richard Rhodes, *John James Audubon: The Making of an American.* 2004.

Rebecca Rischin, *For the End of Time: The Story of the Messiaen Quartet.* 2006.

Julia Rothman, *Nature Anatomy.* 2015.

Allen Shawn, *Arnold Schoenberg's Journey.* 2002.

—————, *Five Piano Sonatas.* Albany CD, 2018.

—————, "Song of the Tango-Bird" on *Sextet and Other Works.* Koch CD, 2020.

—————, Various works on soundcloud.com.

Jonathan D. Silver, "Forever changed," *Pittsburgh Tribune-Review*, January 22, 2023: A1, 4-5.

William Souder, *Under a Wild Sky: John James Audubon and the Making of the "Birds of America."* 2014.

Susan Tichy, *Niedecker's Birds: A Field Guide.* Online.

Alexis de Tocqueville, *Democracy in America.* Transl. Henry Reeve. 2000.

Richard D. White, Jr., *Kingfish: The Reign of Huey P. Long.* 2006.

Heather Woods, *Bundling.* 2022.

David Zinnman, *The Day Huey Long Was Shot.* 1993.

THE TRAINS OF OLD HORNELL

"I detest the clockwork that removes the lines"
—Lisa Robertson's Baudelaire

He can't remember ever hearing a train, tho it was always here

Along with dancing floaters the brain soon trains the eye ignore

The invading blade that opens small gashes of horizontal sound

in the bedroom wall hasn't stopped so far the agony

of Boschwitz's The Passenger which turns out to be

an aching gut of a bedtime read bound to keep him up

A man is riding trains in the book and never getting away

He boards to reboard his nightmare

This has been ongoing since the war

If he stops riding, he dies

falling into the hands of

failing to take the next train

It could be the old trains of Hornell he is hearing

five hours and a lifetime away,

streets he once wandered in love as if in his own hometown,

granted by a temporary inversion in the atmosphere.

The sound, weeks after moving here, of the twice-a-day from Harrisburg

had been already absorbed into his snoring the unfamiliar refrigerator planes

cars on the ambient expressway

All this normalcy changed overnight

Tonight the fascist resurgence liquidating the countryside

makes Otto Silbermann urgent

This is why an exhausted poet can't stop

be he old and

limp as a lyric

by Harry Kemp,

Why he still wakes from sleep intermittently ebullient

to record another word,

Why the few durable lines he's salvaged seem out of place,

a few brown hairs in his white beard.

He pretends the passenger is the lonely poet crossing the borders of sleep and madness eventually running out of ground, the eyes of the state upon him. That makes poetry the train, form that never safely arrives. None of this is in the book. My passenger poet cannot know he is inventing autofiction or else his poetry would become a boat for sinking by Nazi subs and not a train at times a circus train out of Florida or the trainwreck of our poetry that renders him nostalgic Anyhow, passport photos of the poets can be grossly misleading Olson looks small and Keats too tall for the tiny space

And the many forms of poetry make it hard to picture real people moving on the train

He tries to think it closer and he fails as on that early morning coming into Salt Lake standing in the baggage car waiting for his car to roll to a stop shit the train yard could have gone on forever coupling and uncoupling forming new trains one long train of a sentence

He is retired to his bedroom in the very landscape Mencken outs as The Libido for the Ugly

To write expired poems

(nothing can follow "lacerate the eyes")

His money dwindling

Like his days

In some kind of race

He bet big on.

After 3 am, he switches trains at Penn Station Baltimore, and begins to read the "lyrical research" of Lisa Robertson.

Learning to walk the aisles of a train in motion is a clinamen, seat to seat.

Experiments in syntax.

The forms of poetry progress rapidly tho the poet observes he is sitting still

a passenger in a moving train watching the moving train pass on the next track.

He likes the poets best who can read on the train with no dizziness.

He likes the poets who hopped on for the ride with no ticket.

Some cars in the train don't care if they do or do not carry the reader along with them.
He will feel the car's rhythm in his stationary body for a long time afterwards.

His imaginary train stations are universities wherein occur big layovers.
His second-story bedroom seems below the invisible train tracks; he sees

the train pulling forms of cars in fugue across a haunted landscape
does not travel left to right or vice versa but only on and off.

He slept fine on the train in his sleeper with his head pointing the direction ahead.
Sleep is the local elsewhere described to death in travel brochures and motel ratings.

Sleep, when it does come, unfolds into Sonia Delaunay's effulgent accordion quilt Prose of
the Trans-Siberian. Things to do in Hornell:

Experience as caesura   the gaps between train sounds
Attempt to understand grammar

by counting the intervals of silence
Perchance to fall asleep like this to dream

he is counting on having time
to finish reading The Baudelaire Fractal

before passing on the prose poem novel
to his daughter this weekend along with a photo

I've framed Frank O'Hara at home
in his hand-carved chair a year before death.

I wouldn't call that a smile.
He has crossed his legs elegantly

below his resting arms, which quote
the inverted V of the chair legs.

A cigarette burns in his hand. Then she is
quoting a letter from Wallace Stevens

"It does not come to rest but it fits in."
and I see I have already come to my decision

I will layover here
making tomorrow's start.

It Does Not Come To Rest

I write this love as all transition
As f I'm in instinctual flight
—Bernadette Mayer

Everything starts with a wave from the conductor.

All seats in the car face backwards
So looking out the window to pass time already
Whisked away
Like scenery from a set in a play.

I wake from a short nap on the wrong train
Continue falling thru a world of worlds
Parallel tracks
As if into the arms of a raincoat held out for me

My arms fit into the garment worn backwards
And it seems only natural that I embrace the Angel of the elegy,
Bird of the soul,
A dream of poetry that equivocates the day...

I cannot survive my big discovery, startle:
A woman is addressing me, "my life has been a series
Of train wrecks,"
Her voice like the Internet where no one's a stranger.

On our shared bench beneath some mural
Once depicting strong furniture-like women with names like
Commerce and Industry
Displays poor Marsya's flayed skin--restored strips

Nailed to the public wall. A miracle, he wanted to tell her
Into the city he had gone and witnessed
A miracle:
The blind man made his mouth somehow a terminal

For his song's arrivals and departures
On the twin rails of his instruments
Played together!
The god's punishment for this offense,

For playing hell out of the flute and double-flute, sometimes a bird whistle,
Upside
Down,
Was Apollo's skinning alive Roland Kirk

Who had stumbled across the aulos Athena abandoned
After playing made her cheeks puff out
A miracle discovery
Piet Mondrian finding the black lines in his painting were fast.

Painting the double horizontal line late in his life
Put Mondrian's on a yet another track:
Split,
The black line showed color between two new lines!

It is pretty, that is the word, to see
The polished rails reflecting the sky meet at the horizon
Knowing
They remain parallel. Once, a steam 200-ton localmotif could be

Turned around here, in this circle, and headed back into town
Keeping parallel to the river I lived beside that year
I met Duncan
I believed my unwrit poems promised something big, say

Derail Lowell, I see a callow backwardness
Remembering silo chaff in the college town
Street
To get back, after first success, on the fast track

Bigger than me stealing the spike for paperweight
Step walking the ties became an experiment
Finding
His own rhythm free from monotony

Trespassing rusted sidetrack leading to abandoned
Round house, well within shot of Kirk's rail bird
Cry
To stand inside its concrete bowl at perfect center

And breathe word returned to me instantly
Equally amplified from all points on the circle
"FAST!"
It was not echo expected applause

It was a matter of acoustics, I reprise,
Called "the center of the universe,"
Inaudible
To anyone not the speaker.

FINISHED ON THE REOPENING OF THE FERN HOLLOW BRIDGE, DECEMBER 2022

Ziggurat for Mark Spitzer
(1965-2023)

Audubon saw garfish aplenty
  I count five mentions in the L of A—
    They appear always hoping to eat birds.
      Catesby painted the green garfish
A century before hungry Audubon published. Once,
  When a botanist had wandered off,
    Audubon feared
      He'd been eaten by one.

www.ingramcontent.com/pod-product-compliance
Lightning Source LLC
Chambersburg PA
CBHW041516120626
46551CB00018B/2453